My Favorite Anim

I LOVE PANDAS!

By Beth Gottlieb

Gareth Stevens
PUBLISHING

Please visit our website, www.garethstevens.com. For a free color catalog of all our high-quality books, call toll free 1-800-542-2595 or fax 1-877-542-2596.

Library of Congress Cataloging-in-Publication Data
Names: Gottlieb, Beth, author.
Title: I love pandas! / Beth Gottlieb.
Description: Buffalo, New York : Gareth Stevens Publishing, [2023] | Series: My favorite animal | Includes index.
Identifiers: LCCN 2022014029 (print) | LCCN 2022014030 (ebook) | ISBN 9781538283356 (paperback) | ISBN 9781538283370 (library binding) | ISBN 9781538283387 (ebook)
Subjects: LCSH: Pandas–Juvenile literature.
Classification: LCC QL737.C27 G68 2023 (print) | LCC QL737.C27 (ebook) | DDC 599.789–dc23/eng/20220518
LC record available at https://lccn.loc.gov/2022014029
LC ebook record available at https://lccn.loc.gov/2022014030

First Edition

Published in 2023 by
Gareth Stevens Publishing
2544 Clinton St,
Buffalo, NY 14224

Editor: Kristen Nelson
Designer: Rachel Rising

Photo credits: Cover, p. 1 LP2 Studio/Shutterstock.com; p. 5 PHOTO BY LOLA/Shutterstock.com; pp. 7, 11, 19, 21, 24 Hung Chung Chih/Shutterstock.com; p. 9 Wonderly Imaging/Shutterstock.com; p. 13 Philip louis valenzuela/Shutterstock.com; pp. 15, 24 Ninelro/Shutterstock.com; p. 17 Bryan Faust/Shutterstock.com; p. 23 plavi011/Shutterstock.com.

Printed in the United States of America

CPSIA compliance information: Batch #CWGS23: For further information contact Gareth Stevens, New York, New York at 1-800-542-2595.

Find us on

Contents

I love pandas!

They are a kind of bear.

They live in China.
They live in
the mountains.

They are black
and white.

They have thick fur.
It keeps them warm.

Pandas eat one plant.
It is bamboo.

They spend a lot of time eating!

Pandas move slowly.
They are great
tree climbers.

Babies are tiny.
They are called cubs.

Mothers care for cubs.

Words to Know

bamboo   cub   fur

Index